In the Palm of His Hand

poems by

Karen Holmes

Published by Feather Books
PO Box 438
Shrewsbury SY3 0WN, UK
Tel/fax; 01743 872177

Website URL: http://www.waddysweb.freeuk.com
e-mail: john@waddysweb.freeuk.com

2006

I would like to dedicate this book to my Uncle Dave, who would have been proud of me for finally doing something with my dream.

ISBN-10:   1-84175-251-7
ISBN-13: 978-1-84175-251-8

No. 261 in the Feather Books Poetry Series

Contents

Be the Centre. 5

All in the name of Beauty!. 6

Bereavement 8

Keeping up Appearances. 10

Little Old Me. 12

I Don't know all the Answers 14

Meet with Me 16

The Word of God 17

Learning to Fly. 18

Sovereign Lord. 19

My Cherished Ones 20

Live Life 22

Getting By 24

His Grace 26

Peace 28

Author's Note

Thank you to all those people who have believed in me enough to encourage me to publish my poetry. I hope this book will encourage and bless everyone who reads it and perhaps cause people to consider their own faith and where they stand with God.

This is not just about getting my poetry into print, but also an effort to raise money for some of my favourite charities, as a donation will be given for each book sold. Thank you on their behalf for purchasing this book.

I have always loved poetry, even from primary school age and so it was natural to write verse about my family and friends and eventually my experience of God. Life has presented many difficulties along the way and so the poems will reflect the ups and downs of life.

The title represents the fact that it is only when we are held in the palm of God's hand that we can truly be ourselves. It is only when we are captured by His love that we are truly free and when we are in that place of safety, we can praise Him all the more.

Feel free to read the poems in a public setting but please do not reproduce them without prior permission.

Karen Holmes © 2006

BE THE CENTRE

Be the centre of my worship, be my heart's complete devotion.
Block out every distraction, surpass all my own emotion.
May the treasure that's within me bubble through my outer clay,
Let me be your holy temple, come and dwell in me I pray.
Strip away the things that hinder,
For my soul delights to soar to new heights
Upheld by angels
Heaven's glory to explore.

This soul of mine cannot be held in bondage or in chains
For Satan's power was broken when my Jesus rose again.
And though this outer body begins to fade and age,
My spirit laughs and dances upon heaven's stage.
For there's no comprehension by my soul of earthly grind
It's unperturbed by heartache, to disappointment blind.
It's deaf to age restrictions, to ill health it's immune,
My soul is free in Jesus and dances to His tune.

Let's not quash the Spirit or silence any voice,
Don't subdue the jubilant expression
Of all His loving mercy, His overwhelming grace;
Our worship here's an elementary lesson,
For heaven is our homeland, our destiny foretold.
So don't suppress your worship or let your heart grow cold.
Our souls are well aware of the glory that awaits
When finally we're free to enter heaven's gates.

Dancing in the hallways of heaven's promised mansion,
Kneeling at the feet of Christ my Lord,
Worshipping in harmony with choirs of angel voices
Bowing at His throne in silent awe.

ALL IN THE NAME OF BEAUTY!

Surgery, pills, creams, oils and potions,
Face lifts and nose jobs and make up and lotions,
Bottles of colour to hide each grey hair,
Aftershave, perfume, their scents fill the air;
Eye shadow, lipstick, mascara, foundation,
Creams to revive our wrinkly nation,
Smoothers and fillers and shadow concealer,
Injections of botox and acid face peeler;
Sunbeds and fake tan and tooth-whitening pearls,
Bath oil for blokes and bubbles for girls,
Shampoo, conditioner, mousse, wax and gel,
Hair straighteners, curlers and crimpers as well;
Highlights and perms and lowlights I guess
and still I go out with my hair in a mess.

There's shelf loads of products in every store,
Who knows (and who cares?) what they're s'posed to be for;
Results will be stunning, they're all tried and tested
and well worth the money that you have invested;
You'll feel oh so beautiful, look like a dream,
such high expectations from a small jar of cream.

But what of the beauty that's more than skin deep?
A brand new creation can never come cheap.
The old things are past and everything's new,
That's what the power of Jesus can do.
A heart that is cleansed by the blood of the lamb,
A God who accepts me to come as I am.

6

A cleansing that wipes out the guilt and the sin
and all because God saw the state I was in.
We'd all like a miracle, Lord, for today,
Oh please keep us slim, stop our hair going grey;
But better by far than that stuff in a jar
It's deep inner beauty for which I would pray,
A voice that is kind,
A heart of compassion,
A love that endures,
And won't go out of fashion.

Lord, help me spend time on the beauty that matters,
make me a reflection of You.
May the heart of my Jesus, His truth and His wisdom
be seen in the things that I do.

BEREAVEMENT

"Victory is assured to those who believe"

(A poem about the loss of my uncle)

They're safe now, Lord, those we've loved and lost
But yet we cry and still we try to count the cost;
All those times we took for granted,
How we wish that we had counted
Every precious sixty seconds.
Way too late we learn life's lessons.

Those we've loved and lost now feel no pain.
The agony is ours who here on earth remain.
The tears flow unchecked - and checked they flow again.
Our wounds will weep to speak of that which words cannot explain.

They're safe now, Lord, those we've loved and lost
And so are we, if only we could see
Beyond this poor reflection of all that lies in wait
When we too leave this earth, this temporary state,
And fly with all the angels and dance on ageless limbs
On glimpsing heaven's glory, this poor, tired earth grows dim.

Those we've loved and lost now know no tears.
It's we who grieve and mourn their unlived years,
An anguish that proclaims unspoken fears,
Our heart is pierced as if by many spears.

They're safe now, Lord, those we've loved and lost,
And love remains, and memories we keep,
And those we feel have disappeared forever
Are simply out of sight and fast asleep.
We see them not upon our own horizon
But mortal eyesight fails and dims with age,
And on a distant shore they will be welcomed.
Eternal life begins another page.
The completion of this journey, the ending of this chapter
Brings pages yet unread by us, and frees us from the captor -
that we call life - it's all we've known.
Frail bodies into which we've grown
Are temporary dwellings; inside is the treasure
Beyond understanding, beyond our measure.
If only we'd grasp that life's ending brings more
And death's not the future; it's only a door.

They're safe now, Lord, those we've loved and lost,
And in our pain, our anger, disbelief,
Reach out and reassure us in our grief
That just as you embrace us in our pain,
You also hold the ones for whom we cry
And somehow they are not so far away;
For they - and we - are nurtured, Lord, by You.
You hold my hand, and yet you hold theirs, too.

KEEPING UP APPEARANCES

I'm handing it over to you, God,
This thing we call "control."
We've all held on to a bit of ourselves:
A dream, a love, a goal.
We've given you all the rest, God.
"Take all there is of me",
But I'll keep hold
Of a bit of the old,
The person I want to be.

We have to hold on to control, God,
Or the world would knock us flying.
It isn't that we're pretending,
Deliberately lying.
You can have me on a Sunday,
"Take all there is of me",
But the rest of the week
(though your will I seek)
I need to survive, you see.

I want to be filled with your Spirit
But I don't want to lose control.
It's all about keeping appearances,
I'm really a sensitive soul.
So, break me, mould me, make me,
"Take all there is of me"
But let me sit glued to my seat at the back,
I'd look daft if I fell to my knees.

Oh God, how I need to repent
Of holding on firm to the reins.
I'm tying myself up in knots
And I'm binding myself with chains.
Who cares what people might think?
Perhaps it might set *them* free.
Lord, come and take full control now,
"Take all there is of me"

LITTLE OLD ME

I'm created for Your purpose
But I feel so unprepared.
I step outside my comfort zone
And suddenly I'm scared.

You really should know better, God,
I'm not the one you need.
There's loads of other Christians,
Use someone else, I plead.

Somebody more outspoken,
Someone who has more nerve,
Find me a quiet corner
And gladly there I'll serve.

It was all very well when you called me,
I was feeling brave and strong,
But now I'm beginning to wonder,
Maybe I heard You wrong.

Perhaps it's all a big mistake
You meant to call someone else,
Somebody clever and learned,
Or someone with better health.

Oh Lord, I'm clutching at straws now
And any excuse will do;
I'm created for your purpose,
But how can I serve You?

I'm just me, Lord, just little old me,
And I wish You'd understand
You need someone greater than me
For this task that you have planned.

Ask anyone - they'll tell you.
You made a most foolish choice,
Yet still in the back of my mind
I can hear your patient voice.

"Yes I am your Creator, there's nothing I don't know.
I planned each detail of your life - the way that you should go.

When you look in the mirror you see the outer shell,
but I can see the inner you - the one I know so well.

And you have no idea of the things that I have planned
If you let me lead you forward, if you take hold of my hand.
You're pointing out your weaknesses
but in them I am strong;
So step outside your comfort zone
and let me prove you wrong."

I DON'T KNOW ALL THE ANSWERS

I'm trying to make sense of unfathomable things,
I'm attempting to fit all the pieces;
It's a lifetime puzzle of multiple options
and each day the conundrum increases.

The picture starts coming together
But there's pieces as yet still unseen;
Suggestions, ideas, possibilities,
But how do I know what they mean?

I've tried to make informed decisions,
Good, bad, indifferent - who knows?
But I cannot help asking questions
Of the way that this life sometimes goes.

Questions of struggles between right and wrong,
Conflicts of heart and of soul,
Battles which threaten to tear us apart,
Feelings that seek to control;
Illness and death and sorrow and pain,
Loss and bereavement and grief,
Famine and drought and disaster,
Things which would rock our belief.

Glib answers are empty and useless.
The world turns away with a sigh.
So sometimes I have to be honest
and admit that I don't know why

I don't know the answer to most of life's questions
But I know Him in whom I believe
and His plans and purposes find their fulfilment
In ways that I cannot conceive.
I don't need to know all the details
I am safe for He has full control
He will finish the work He has started
I can say, "It is well with my soul."

MEET WITH ME

In me, God, somewhere there's an ache, a yearning,
A searching for something which I cannot quite describe.
An emptiness, an unfulfilled desire,
A conviction that there's more to be had,
A richness that my inadequate groping in the dark has not yet touched.

It has nothing to do with being religious.
Mere ceremony and repetitious words leave me cold.
It is Spiritual - on a level as old as the world itself,
A basic, uncomplicated, sincere, longing for You.

But who are you? Creator, Teacher, Saviour.
My intellect is unable to grasp even a fragment of
Your Splendour and Holiness.
But my spirit aches for your presence.

Sometimes I catch a glimpse of your Power and Majesty.
Sometimes I can reach out and touch heaven's glory.
There is a oneness, a sense of being complete,
A moment of being whole.

Come, O God, and meet with me.
Accept me in my poverty and bestow upon me the richness of Your
Love.
Fill that empty part of me until I overflow with your beauty.
I find no contentment, no satisfaction, no fulfilment
save in You.

THE WORD OF GOD

(Based upon Deuteronomy, Chapter 6: verses 4-9)

Impress My Word upon your heart
And wear upon your hands
The statutes of your God and King
As on those laws you stand.

Take hold of all that I command
And bind it to yourself;
Make it a very part of you
Not just a bible on a shelf -

But a living, vibrant, power-filled source
Of all your inspiration,
A walking, breathing, open book,
Make me your conversation.

Write my laws around your house
Upon your gates and doors;
Don't experience me second hand
But claim my truth as yours.

Write My Word upon your heart
Make it an integral part
Of your routine daily living,
Heed the laws which I am giving.

Impress them on your children
Talk about me each day;
Wherever you are, whatever you do,
Make me a part of all you say and all you do.
Love the Lord with all your heart
and know that I love you.

LEARNING TO FLY

I want to fly, Lord, I want to soar,
I want to be lost in wonder and awe,
I want to see you, reach out and touch
the hem of your garment; am I asking too much?

I want to dance, Lord, I want to run –
Into your presence, I want to have fun;
I come as a child, O God, set me free,
A brand new creation is my destiny.

I want to climb, Lord, reaching new heights,
I want to see visions, O give me fresh sight;
Lord open my eyes and my mind and my heart,
I want to be holy, for you set apart.

I want to drink only the water of life,
Eat manna sent down from on high
I want to be filled by the Spirit of God,
Rise up like an eagle and fly;
I'm no longer bound by the things of the past,
No longer defeated by shame,
For Jesus redeemed me by dying on the cross
and victoriously rising again.

Now sin has been cancelled and chains have been broken
and Satan is powerless for Jesus has spoken;
Now life has been given and death has no sting,
How can I not dance? How can I not sing?

Yes life brings its heartache, still sometimes I cry
But just for the moment - I'm learning to fly!

SOVEREIGN LORD

(Based on Ezekiel Chapter 34, verses: 11-16.)

I myself will search for the sheep who have been scattered
I myself will care for them again;
As a shepherd I will search for those who are abandoned;
I myself will tend the sick and lame.
I will be their rescuer, retrieving them from darkness,
Gathering them and leading them onto higher ground.
I will tend them in good pasture, in rich pasture they will dwell;
I will not stop till every one is found

I myself will give them rest, in safety will they graze;
I will bind up all their wounds and bring back all who've strayed;
The weak shall be made strong again, justice will be restored;
I myself will be their shepherd, I the sovereign Lord.

O Sovereign Lord, today we place ourselves back in your care;
Forgive us for our wanderings, our damaged lives repair.
Rescue us from the darkness of this land that's lost it's way;
Return us to the safety of your pasture, Lord, we pray;
Bind up the broken hearted and hear our feeble cry;
Be strong in all our weaknesses, save us or we die.

I myself will search for the sheep who have been scattered;
I myself will care for you again;
As a shepherd I will search for those who are abandoned;
I myself will tend the sick and lame.
I will be your rescuer, retrieving you from darkness,
Gathering you and leading you onto higher ground.
I will tend you in good pasture, in rich pasture you will dwell
I will not stop till every one is found.

I myself will give you rest, in safety you will graze;
I will bind up all your wounds and bring back all who've strayed;
The weak will be made strong again, justice will be restored
I myself will be your shepherd, I the sovereign Lord.

(This poem came to life as a particular word for the fellowship to which I belong. A message of love, challenge and hope from Father God. I feel it is right to include it here to bring the same message to all who read it.)

MY CHERISHED ONES

In my greatness, in my power
In my all consuming might,
I would dwell in you, my people,
You are precious in my sight.

Not in weakness, not in fear.
Not in brokenness or pain.
But in overwhelming glory
I will build you up again.

Come and pause in utter stillness.
In the silence let me speak.
In this time of pure submission
Every heart will hear me speak

'Stop the noise, confusion cease!
Holy Spirit's power release.
Tongues of fire upon you fall.
I have heard your desperate call.

Don't deny your desperation, take my offered full Salvation.
Let My Spirit settle now, stand or kneel or weep or bow.
Don't deny My Spirit's voice; do you think you're here by choice?
Called and chosen, picked, appointed, individually anointed,
Oil from heaven's heart is flowing, the river of My Spirit's growing -
Overwhelming, flowing free. Sparkling life to you from Me

Do not question what I say,
Do not look the other way,
Do not say it's not for you,
Do not question what I do.
Don't get busy, working hard in a bid to disregard -
Something which you can't explain - do you think I'll die again?

Do you think more could be done than the death of Jesus, Son
Of God and King of Kings?
Would you turn and worship things
Of earth - such dross, such fading treasure -
When I bring life that has no measure?
Will you settle for something less than all that I would seek to bless
You with? My Spirit hovers here.
I see the earth so full of fear
And you, my cherished, loved possession,
Let me hear your heart's confession,
Let me hear your souls deep plea,
Let me see your thirst for me.
I delight in your desire for my Holy burning fire.

In my greatness, in my power,
In my all consuming might,
I would dwell in you, My people,
You are precious in My sight.

Not in weakness, not in fear,
Not in brokenness or pain,
But in overwhelming glory
I will build you up again.

LIVE LIFE

I can live in my yesterdays, memories faded,
Live for past victories, now tired and jaded,
Dance at my joyfulness, weep at my pain,
Relive every moment all over again.
Recalling the facts just like school day revision,
Question my judgement, review each decision,
Rearrange scenes, conversations, events,
Swap things around till they somehow make sense.
But I can't rewrite history, try as I might;
There's no way of returning, making everything right.
I often imagine and sometimes I dream
Of turning the clock back to wipe the slate clean.
But what of the past would I really erase?
There's much that is precious in my yesterdays.
By deleting the pain, the heartache and sorrow
I might change my history and spoil my tomorrow.

I can live for the future when dreams will come true,
I can plan my tomorrows and what I will do.
Imagined success puts today's needs on hold
I'll get my life sorted before I grow old.
One day fate will deal me the cards that I seek
To bring about change and to make life complete.
I'm waiting for something, I'm not sure what,
But till then I cannot enjoy what I've got.
I'm aiming much higher, my future awaits;
Yet sometimes I'm scared that it might arrive late.

Tomorrow or next week is not guaranteed,
Each year seems to pass at a much greater speed;
And so I must ask, can I really afford
To waste my todays though they may appear flawed?
To live in the future demands a high price.
I lay down my "nows" and today sacrifice.

I can live in the present and claim what is mine
For the deeds of this hour shape my future's design.
Yesterdays lessons hold true for today,
Building foundations and paving the way
For me to achieve the desires of my heart;
I'll make today count for the future must start
With now, with this moment, I will not delay,
I'll live to the full every hour of today.

GETTING BY

I know how to "get by" God;
it's something I've achieved
by letting go of futile dreams
in which I once believed.
I've thought so many times, God,
that the goal-post was in view
but someone always moves it
so, "get by" is what I do.
There's no great satisfaction,
no energetic zeal,
no all consuming passion,
life's not such a big deal.

This getting by isn't living,
it's boring and it's dull;
You promised us abundant life
rich and meaningful.
God shake me from my slumber
and wake me from my sleep.
Let me dance with joy at life
and mourn with those who weep.
Strip away indifference
let apathy depart.
Restore to me the joy
of Your Salvation in my heart.

And recreate those dreams, Lord,
and resurrect my soul.
Give me a new direction
a purpose and a goal.
Rekindle fires of passion,
a life that shines for You.
Stir up those dying embers
until they burn anew.
Bring streams of living water
and cleanse me from my sin.
Then fill me with Your Spirit
till I can't keep it in.
Pour out a new anointing.
Refresh me and restore.
Equip me with Your power
and guide and use me more.

Lord, open heaven's floodgates
and pour out from above
a new and mighty measure
of Your all surpassing love.
I turn, Lord, from my unbelief,
repent of every sin,
and fix my eyes on Jesus
for life is found in Him.

HIS GRACE

Beyond my comprehension,
Outside of time and space,
Surpassing expectations,
The wonder of God's grace.

Riches beyond measure,
Treasure for our dross,
Full and free salvation,
Christ's victory on the cross.

Mercy in our failings,
Healing for our pain,
Love that knows no limits,
Power in Jesus' name.

The darkness cannot hide Him.
No sin outweighs His grace.
No cloud can shade His glory.
What can we do but praise?

No human mind can fathom.
No man can understand
how perfect are the blessings
which flow from God's own hand.

It's grace that heals the broken.
It's grace that sets us free.
It's grace that makes us worthy.
His grace in you and me.

The way has now been opened
God doesn't hide His face,
For Jesus conquered sin and death
and brought us to this place

Where we can boldly venture
before God's holy throne;
forgiven and accepted,
our names by Him are known.

Without Him we'd be truly lost,
we could not run the race;
Each day depend and wholly lean
on God's unfailing grace.

PEACE

Peace demonstrations we see on our screens,
Strongly voiced statements and loud, ugly scenes.
I wonder, do any of us know what peace means?
And where can we find it outside of our dreams?

If all politicians refused to wage war
Would people respect and obey every law?
Or maybe they'd find something else to fight for.
There's always been conflicts; there'll be many more.

For even in "peace time" there's anger and strife.
It's part of our culture and part of our life.
We talk of our battles, wishing they'd cease,
Forgetting that Jesus has offered us peace.

A peace unaffected by outward events,
No external forces can shake;
A peace that allows me to sleep through the night
And holds me the moment I wake.

There are no guarantees in this life we will find,
Yet God holds this world in His hands,
And when all our moments are trusted to Him
He leads us in ways He has planned.

His peace is beyond understanding.
We stand, though our world falls apart.
This earth is our temporary dwelling.
Our future is held in God's heart.